Crochet Lessons for Left-Handers

Step By Step Guide for Beginners

Copyright © 2021

All rights reserved.

DEDICATION

The author and publisher have provided this e-book to you for your personal use only. You may not make this e-book publicly available in any way. Copyright infringement is against the law. If you believe the copy of this e-book you are reading infringes on the author's copyright, please notify the publisher at: https://us.macmillan.com/piracy

Contents

Acknowledge... *1*

How to Learn Left-Handed Crochet *1*

Left Handed – Method of How to Knit *5*

Method 1- Mastering the Basics of Left-Handed Crocheting
.... **10**

Method 2- Using Patterns as a Left-Handed Crocheter **15**

Step-by-Step Left-Handed Crochet Patterns *17*

   A Magic Ring (Left-Handed) *17*

   Crochet Chain Left-Handed *24*

   Crochet Scrunchie Pattern *29*

   Eco-Friendly Cosmetic Rounds *31*

   Crochet Plant Hanger *38*

   Twisted Chain Bangle *45*

Acknowledge

Left handed crocheters may find it a challenge to learn the basics and follow patterns when everything seems to be geared towards right handed crocheters. Learning more about left handed crocheting can be helpful whether you are just getting started or looking for way to make crocheting left handed easier for you.

How to Learn Left-Handed Crochet

Left-handed crochet is as common as the number of people who are naturally left-handed. In spite of this, most crochet instructions are written for right-handed crafters. As a leftie, it can feel like the craft world has left you out. Luckily, that's changing, thanks to a number of motivated designers who have created tutorials and patterns for left-handed crafters. Even without those resources, though, it doesn't have to be difficult to learn how to crochet left-handed. The following resources and tips will get you started.

- There's No "Right" Way to Learn

The first thing you need to know is that everyone crochets a little differently. So, there is no one "correct" way of doing it; there are many possible variations of correct when it comes to crochet. This is true or not you are left-handed.

One of the things that people do differently when learning how to crochet is that they hold their crochet hook a certain way. People often use either a "knife grip" or a "pencil grip" but may have their own variations of either one. Left-handed crocheters are no more likely to use one type of grip over the other in comparison with right-handed crocheters.

- Right vs. Left: What's the Difference?

The only real difference between left-handed and right-handed crochet is what hand you hold the hook in and which direction you work a row. In right-handed crochet, the hook is held in the right hand. With a few exceptions for specific niches of crochet, the right-handed crafter works stitches from the right to the left. In left-handed crochet, it's the exact opposite: hold the hook in the left hand and work the stitches from left to right.

- How to Learn

There are a few common ways that people go about learning left-handed crochet:

Follow left-handed crochet tutorials: These are readily available online and include both written tutorials with photos and video tutorials. Many people prefer video tutorials when first learning crochet.

Have a left-handed crafter teach you: Ask at your local craft store if there is a crochet teacher who is available to teach a left-handed crafter.

Sit opposite a right-handed crochet teacher: This will allow you to follow what they are doing while working as the mirror image using your left hand.

Learn to crochet right-handed: This used to be the only option. It's not a top choice for most people, but it's an option. If you're ambidextrous or find that you can easily crochet right-handed even though you're a lefty then it's always an option to just learn "regular" crochet.

It is worth noting that you will be using both hands in crochet regardless of which hand holds the hook. The dominant hand typically holds the hook, but the non-dominant hand stays busy working the yarn and holding the work-in-progress.

- Reverse Images in Graphic Crochet

When working with written crochet patterns, you don't need to do anything differently as a left-handed crocheter. However, when you are working from crochet graphs and charts, you will want to reverse the image before beginning crochet. If you don't, then your left-handed crochet work will have an image that is the opposite of intended. That can be okay with symmetrical images but doesn't work for words and asymmetrical images.

- Teaching Left-Handed Crochet

As a teacher, you can adapt your own crochet style to other-handed crafters. As mentioned before, one option is to sit across from the crafter so that they can mirror your style.

Left Handed – Method of How to Knit

Many left-handed people are convinced that they can't learn to knit. Others think they have to learn a complicated mirror-image type of knitting that involves working the stitches from the right-hand needle onto the left-hand needle.

It's certainly fine to learn and use this method of left-handed knitting if that's what you're comfortable with. However, the truth is that it doesn't need to be that difficult.

Knitting Uses Both Hands

No matter which hand is your dominant hand, both hands are

used in knitting. That's due to the simple fact that there are two needles involved. Right-handed people can use their left hands when knitting, and left-handed people can use their right hands in the same way.

Some left-handed people find it easier to learn the continental method of knitting. The yarn is held in and manipulated by the left hand, which may seem more natural. It is possible to learn the English knitting method as a leftie, too. You may want to practice both to find out which style is right for you.

Just like right-handed people, you will need to practice in order for knitting to feel comfortable and natural. If you're a left-handed person, you might find it best to try the continental method before you try to learn what's known as left-handed knitting.

Learn Left-Handed Knitting

If you gave continental knitting a shot and want to learn left-handed knitting instead, there are great resources online. As you research it, you'll also find many different approaches as well.

Many find the best way to learn is from a fellow leftie who has been where you are now. Unless you know someone personally who is willing to teach you, there are a few places that offer great advice.

One such website is appropriately called Left Handed Knitter. It is run by Karen Lynn, who has dedicated her entire blog to this topic. The archives are deep and offer a wealth of knowledge for new and experienced knitters alike. From the basic stitches to advanced topics like reading charts and finding left-handed cable needles, any obstacle you find in your knitting is probably answered there.

Another great option is to take an online class. One such class, called Left Handed Knitting, is taught by Rick Mondragon—both a lefty and a professional knitter with four decades of experience. The class runs you through the basics and you can work at your own pace, so it's a great way to get started.

Of course, there are a number of differences in left-handed knitting, but two keys to keep in mind as you learn are:

You need to reverse any shaping in the pattern.

When reading charts, you will read from right to left (left to right is taught to right-handers).

Start Knitting

The most important thing to remember is that if you truly want to knit, you can. Everyone feels awkward those first few times they pick up needles, but if you stick with it, you'll get it.

No matter which approach you take, start with a goal of a simple garter stitch scarf and just keep working the knit stitch over and over again until you run out of yarn. Then, move to a stockinette scarf and practice purling while fine-tuning your knit stitch.

Those two projects should give you plenty of time to hone your skills and it doesn't matter how the scarves turn out. The point is that you're developing the muscle memory that all knitters get over time. Before you know it, you may even join the ranks of the yarn obsessed and be teaching other lefties how to knit.

Method 1- Mastering the Basics of Left-Handed Crocheting

1. Hold the hook in your left hand. To crochet left-handed, you will need to hold the hook in your left hand and use your right hand to hold your work. Grip the crochet hook with your left hand so that your thumb and forefinger are gripping the flat part of the hook.
2. Practice chaining. Chaining is how you start your foundation for a crochet project and it is the simplest technique in crocheting. Start by looping the yarn over your index finger twice. Then, pull the second loop through the first loop. This will create a slipstitch. Next, slide this loop on your hook and loop the free end of your yarn over the hook. Pull this new yarn through the loop on the hook to make another loop.

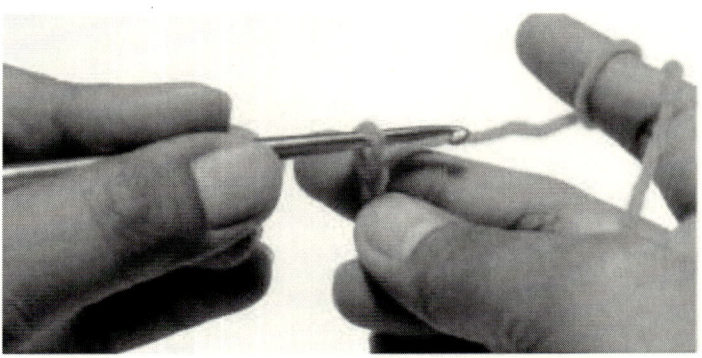

Continue to yarn over and pull the yarn through to form loops. This will create a chain.

Make the chain as long as it needs to be for your project.

Chaining is often abbreviated as "ch."

3. Do a slipstitch. A slipstitch is also sometimes called a joining stitch. To slipstitch, insert the hook through a stitch, and then yarn over. Pull this new yarn through the stitch to complete the slipstitch.

A slipstitch may be used to move from one location to another on your yarn, or it may be used to join two stitches together, such as when you are crocheting in the round.

4. Try a single crochet. A single crochet stitch is another simple

stitch that often comes up in patterns. To single crochet, insert the hook through the stitch, yarn over, and then pull this new yarn through the two stitches on the hook. Then, yarn over again and pull the yarn through the two loops on the hook.

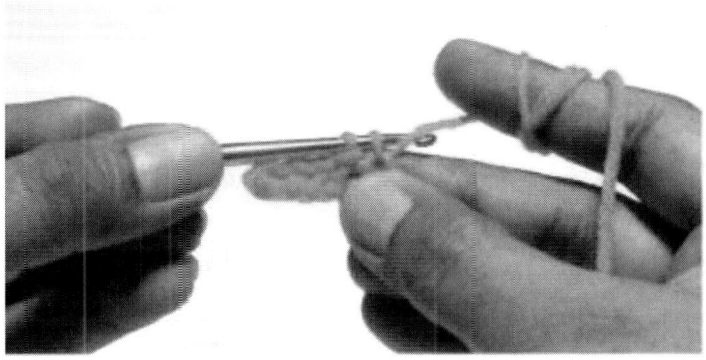

A single crochet stitch is usually abbreviated as "sc."

5. Do a double crochet. Double crochet stitches are also quite common. To double crochet, yarn over the hook, then insert the hook through the stitch and yarn over again. Then, pull through the first stitch, and yarn over again. Then, pull through the first two stitches and yarn over again. Pull through the last two stitches to complete the stitch.

Double crochet is usually abbreviated as "dc."

6. Try a half double crochet. Half double crochet is not as common, but it is important to know for more advanced work. A half-double crochet stitch is done by yarning over and then inserting the hook into the stitch. Then, yarning over again and pulling through three stitches. Then, yarn over again and pull through three stitches again.

Half-double crochet is usually abbreviated as "hdc."

7. Attempt a triple crochet. A triple crochet stitch is also not as common, but it is important to learn. To do a triple crochet stitch, start by yarning over twice. Then, insert the hook into the stitch and yarn over again. Next, pull the yarn through four loops and yarn over again. Then, pull through two loops and yarn over again. Then, pull through two loops again and yarn over one more time. Then, pull through the last two loops to finish the stitch.

A triple crochet stitch is usually abbreviated in patterns with "tr."

8. Crochet in the round. Crocheting in the round is the same when you are left handed as well. Start by making a chain, and then secure it in a circle with a slipstitch.[8] Then, continue to work your stitches into the chain. You can crochet in the round to create hats, heavy scarves, and cowls.
9. Experiment with special stitches. There are many different types of stitches that you can use to create interesting patterns in your crocheted work. Once you feel comfortable with the basic stitches, you can try out some more advanced ones. Some stitches you might like to try include:

- Shell stitch
- Popcorn stitch
- Box stitch

Method 2- Using Patterns as a Left-Handed Crocheter

1. Seek out left-handed tutorials. Having reference pictures can be helpful when following pattern or learning a new stitch, but many of the tutorials you will find are made for right-handed crocheters. However, there are lots of left-handed picture and video tutorials available, so seek them out.

Check out blogs and videos made by other left handed crocheters.

You might even consider getting yourself a left handed crocheter pattern book.

2. Follow the pattern as usual. Crocheting left-handed does not mean that you can't use the same patterns as right-handed crocheters. Follow the pattern instructions exactly as they are written. Just use your left hand to crochet the stitches.
3. Take pictures of images and flip them. One of the difficult parts of using tutorials when you are a left-handed crocheter is that the images usually show a right-handed crocheter.

One way to change the image into something you can try to do with your left hand is to save the images and then flip them horizontally. This will reverse the image so that it looks like the crocheter is left handed.

Step-by-Step Left-Handed Crochet Patterns

A Magic Ring (Left-Handed)

Doesn't that look nice? The lack of hole makes the Magic Ring a great choice for amigurumi.

What is a Magic Ring?

A Magic Ring is a great way to to begin a crochet project that will be worked in the round. This technique is excellent for amigurumi. It is also called an Adjustable Ring, Magic Loop, Magic Circle, and Make Circle.

When can a Magic Ring be used?

It can be used on any project that is worked in rounds. It works for both crocheting in a continuous spiral and in joined rounds. Use it instead of "Ch 2, x sc in 2nd ch from hook" in patterns.

Why should I use a Magic Ring?

It's easy and it looks good! One of the biggest benefits of using a Magic Ring is that there is no hole in the beginning of your work. The following photo shows the difference between "Ch 2, 6 sc in 2nd ch from hook" and 6 sc into a Magic Ring

Can a Magic Ring only be used with single crochet stitches? Nope. Single crochet (sc), half-double crochet (hdc), double crochet (dc), triple crochet (tr), and more, can all be used with a Magic Ring.

So, how do I make a Magic Ring?

1. Loop yarn around with working yarn on top. Alternatively, you could loop yarn around your fingers to start.

2. Insert crochet hook into loop. Hook working yarn… I usually hold onto where the yarn crosses with my thumb like I am in picture 3, but I am not doing so in pictures 2 and 4 so you can better see what is going on.

3. …pull working yarn through loop…

4. …and pull yarn up. You now have 1 loop on hook.

5. Yarn over and pull through loop on hook to chain 1.

6. This counts as ch 1, not a sc. You are now ready to crochet into ring.

In this tutorial, I am crocheting 6 single crochet stitches into the Magic Ring. It is often written as "6 sc into a Magic Ring". Many patterns worked in the round start with 6 stitches, but not all. Crochet as many stitches as the pattern states to do.

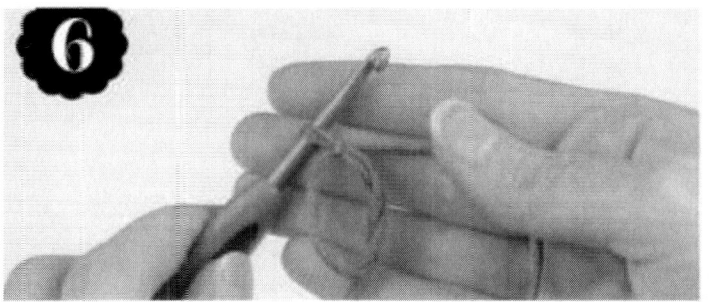

Other stitches:

Half-Double Crochet – Start crocheting hdc into ring the same as you would sc. I know what you are thinking, "Aren't you supposed to ch 2 when starting hdc?". In rows, yes. For rounds, I prefer only 1 ch. It is a preference, you can do either.

Double Crochet – Ch 2 more times, you have now made 3 chains and this will count as your first dc stitch. Begin crocheting dc into ring

Triple Crochet – Ch 3 more times, you have now made 4

chains and this will count as your first tr stitch. Begin crocheting tr into ring.

7. Insert hook into ring, yarn over and pull through ring.

8. You now have 2 loops on hook.

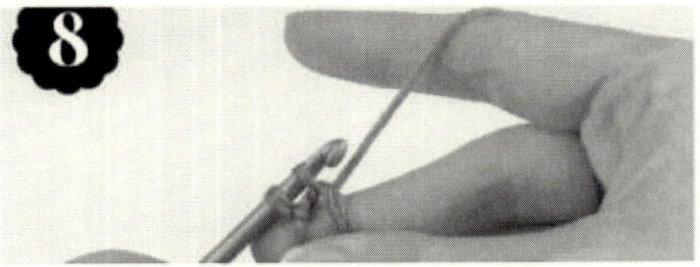

9. Yarn over and pull through both loops.

10. You now have 1 sc in your ring. Continue until you have the number of stitches needed for pattern.

11. Once you have completed all your stitches, you'll pick up the yarn tail with your hand…

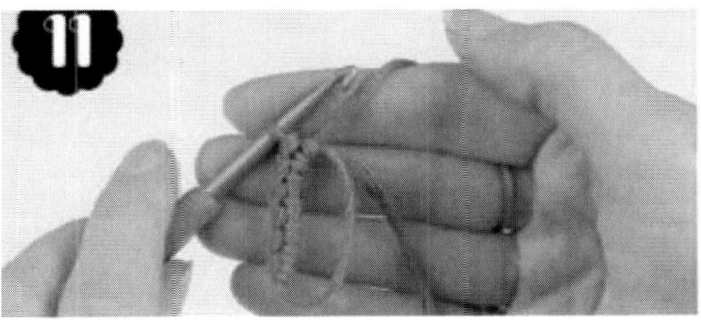

12. ...and pull until the ring closes.

13. Completed ring!

If you are working in a continuous spiral, sc into the first stitch you made in round 1. If you are working in joined rounds, slip stitch in first sc of round 1 to join.

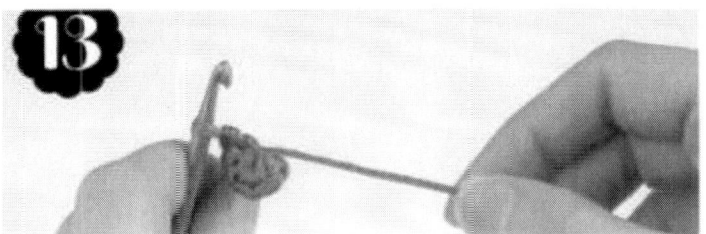

HOW TO KEEP THE HOLE CLOSED.

Depending on the type of yarn you are using, the hole may widen as you continue to crochet. I find this is more likely to happen with slippery yarns made from materials such as acrylic, nylon, or silk. Here are 3 ways to keep the hole closed:

1. If you will not see the backside of the project, after you have completed the second round, pull yarn tail tight. Using a yarn needle, tie off yarn through the backside of a stitch. This technique is great for amigurumi. Once you have tied the knot, you just leave the yarn tail inside.

2. If you will see the backside of the finished project, weave the yarn tail in as soon as you have enough rounds completed to do so. You may need to tighten the hole again before weaving by pulling on the yarn tail.

3. You can crochet over the yarn tail while crocheting round 2. Note: I do not like this technique for amigurumi because it will increase the stitch height of round 2. This may be fine for something like a hat, but it can change the shape noticeably of something delicate like an animal's nose.

Crochet Chain Left-Handed

1. Begin with a slip knot.
2. Yarn over. Note that every time you "yarn over" in your crochet work, you will be scooping the yarn clockwise with your hook to pick up the yarn.
3. Draw hook through loop. You'll scoop the yarn clockwise here.
4. Repeat steps 2-3; each repetition is one chain.

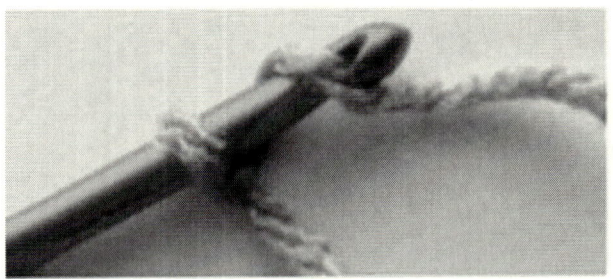

HOW TO SINGLE CROCHET LEFT-HANDED

1. Crochet a foundation chain of any length.
2. Insert hook into second chain from hook. Your hook will be held in your left hand, the chain will be extending out to the right, and you will insert the hook into the second chainthat is to the right of the hook. This photo demonstrates how you'll go into the chain with your hook, so you have 2 stands on top of the hook and 1 below.

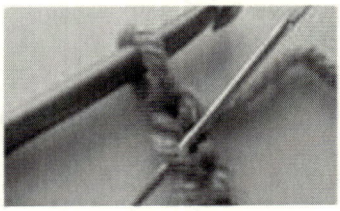 

3. Yarn over.
4. Draw through loop. You will see two loops on your hook at the end of this step.

5. Yarn over.

6. Draw through both loops on hook. This is your first sc.

7. Insert hook into next chain and repeat steps 3-6.

8. Repeat step 7 across row.

HOW TO DOUBLE CROCHET LEFT-HANDED

1. Crochet a foundation chain of any length.

2. Yarn over.

3. Insert hook into fourth chain from hook. This is the fourth chain towards the right, working from left to right away from your hook.

4. Yarn over.

5. Draw through loop. You will see three loops on your hook at the end of this step.

6. Yarn over and draw through the first two of those three loops on the hook.

 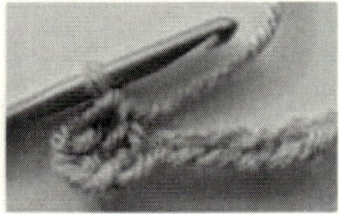

7. Yarn over and draw through the two loops now on the hook. You've completed your first double crochet.
8. Yarn over and insert crochet hook into the next stitch then repeat steps 4-7 for the next stitch.
9. Repeat step 8 across row.
10. Turn work. Chain 3 for turning chain.
11. Yarn over and insert hook into next stitch.
12. In the photo above, I show that you are crocheting your next stitch into the 3rd chain of the turning chain from the previous row. "This ensures stitch count remains correct and shape is not triangular; I made plenty of accidental 'bunting' when I was learning!" Repeat your dc stitches across the entire row.

IMPORTANT TIPS FOR LEFT-HANDED CROCHET

- Leave your beginning yarn tail hanging at the start of each project (don't crochet over it); when a pattern mentions the "right side" or "wrong side" of the work, look for that tail as a cue. The "right side" will be when the tail is on the bottom right corner.
- Remember that every time you yarn over, you are going to "scoop the yarn clockwise". Rachel says that she repeated this mantra to herself regularly when first learning to crochet.
- Left-handed crochet is possible to do with both written patterns and visual ones. With charts and graphs, you can reverse the image (see below in the section on adapting existing patterns) and use the reversed image as your guide.

Crochet Scrunchie Pattern

This crochet Scrunchie is super quick and easy to make. It's the perfect stash buster or a quick make for instant satisfaction. The great thing about these scrunchies is that you can customise them to your liking. Today I have used Bernat Velvet yarn because I love the look and feel and think its a little softer on the hair, but of course, you can choose to use any yarn you like!

MATERIALS AND TOOLS NEEDED

Yarn used: Bernat Velvet in Shadow Purple

Hook: 6.5mm

Hair Ties

CROCHET TERMS

Slip Stitch(s): ss(s): Insert hook, yarn over pull through stitch and loop on hook

Chain(s): ch(s): Yarn over, pull through

Treble Crochet(s): tr(s): Yarn over, insert into stitch, yarn over, pull up a loop, you will have three loops on the hook. Yarn over, pull through two loops, yarn over, pull through remaining two loops.

CROCHET SCRUNCHIE PATTERN

You will be working around the hair tie as you go, this will mean you will insert your hook around the bobble instead of working into a stitch. It might sound complicated, but trust me, it's super easy.

Starting w a slip knot on your hook, dc around hair tie, ch 2

Work 65 tr around hair tie, ss in ch-2 from beginning of the round. Tie off

Weave in ends being careful not to pull too tight. I always use the rule of three.

You can access to this video for step-by-step learning how to crochet scrunchie (left-handed)

https://www.youtube.com/watch?v=F8-YLy3Kw4U&feature=emb_title

Eco-Friendly Cosmetic Rounds

Use these washable rounds anywhere you'd use a disposable cotton round or facial wipe – for cleansing, toning, or removing makeup – and save money while helping the environment! They crochet up in minutes, take very little yarn, and make a pretty and practical gift.

Crochet Lessons for Left-Handers

Terminology

ch   chain

ch-sp   chain space

sc   single crochet (double crochet for UK/Aus)

sl st   slip stitch

st   stitch

You will need…

H US/5mm crochet hook (see *Gauge*, below)

Small quantity of worsted weight cotton yarn.

Yarn needle to weave in ends

Stitch marker

General Instructions

After Round 1, you'll be working in linen stitch (a 'ch 1, sc' repeat).

After Round 2, you'll always work into the chain spaces of the previous round, instead of the stitches, until the final (edging) round, where you'll work a round of slip stitches into each chain space and each single crochet stitch from the previous round.

To begin each linen stitch round, make the first ch 1, then slip your start-of-round stitch marker around the entire chain stitch you've just made (below, left). This will mark the position of the first chain space to work into at the start of the following round (below, right).

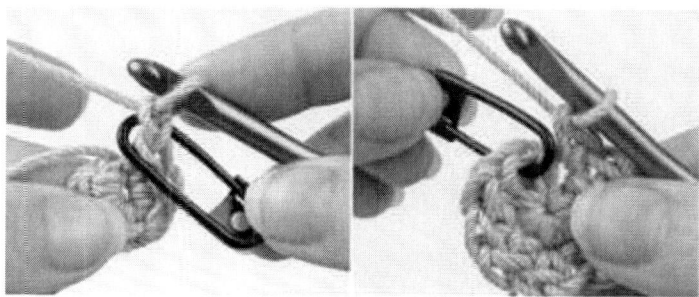

To make slip stitches that aren't too tight:

Do not draw up a loop and immediately pull it through the loop on your hook (below, left) – this will make your sl sts too tight, so the edging will pull in.

Instead, draw up a loop and pull it right up to the height of the loop on your hook (below, right), then draw it through the loop on your hook to complete the slip stitch. Your sl sts will perfectly match the size of your other stitches.

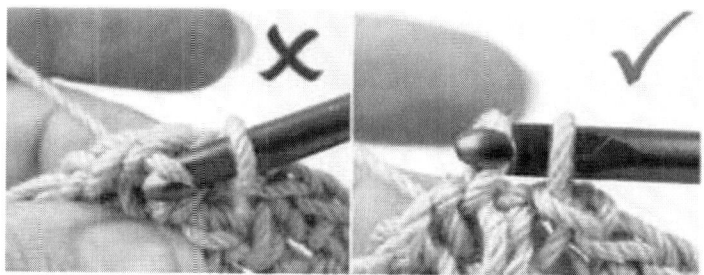

Position of the slip stitches for the edging:

Working into the chain spaces and the stitches around the edge can be tricky – if you accidentally insert your hook in the wrong place when you aim for the chain space, you then won't have anywhere to insert your hook to make the next stitch.

Look at the ch-sp (below, left). You'll see the sideways 'V's belonging to two stitches sitting above the space:

First, the V of the chain (A)

After that, the V of the sc (B)

If you pull up on the chain (A), you'll see a vertical bar in the middle of the space, between A and B (marked by pink arrow, below, right).

Insert your hook before that bar to make the sl st into the ch-sp, and after that bar to make the sl st into the next sc.

Then continue to the next ch-sp and repeat!

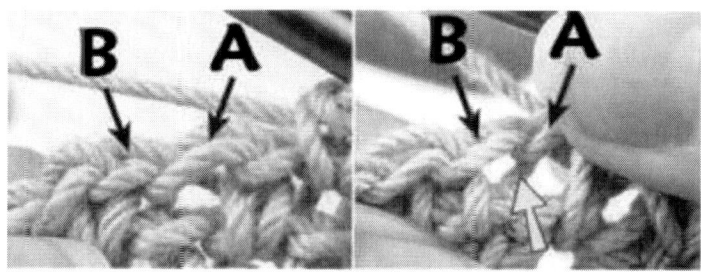

Pattern

Note: *Please see the General Instructions, above, in conjunction with this pattern.*

Make a magic ring, ch 1.

Rnd 1: 6 sc in magic ring. (6 st)

Rnd 2: (ch 1, sc) in each st around. (12 st)

Rnd 3: *(ch 1, sc, ch 1, sc) in next ch-sp, (ch 1, sc) in next ch-sp; repeat from * twice more. (18 st)

Rnd 4: *(ch 1, sc, ch 1, sc) in next ch-sp, (ch 1, sc) in next 2 ch-sp; repeat from * twice more. (24 st)

Rnd 5: *(ch 1, sc, ch 1, sc) in next ch-sp, (ch 1, sc) in next 3 ch-sp; repeat from * twice more. (30 st)

Rnd 6: sl st in each ch-sp and each sc around. (30 st)

Cut the yarn leaving a 3" (8cm) tail, join with an invisible finish, and weave in the ends securely.

After weaving in the ends, flatten the pad with your hand. You'll see that the slip stitch round has smoothed out the edge into a circle (below, left) and given the pad a nice thickness at the edge (below, right).

I hope you enjoy this pattern.

Crochet Plant Hanger

Pot Holder

The pot holder will be worked from the top down, starting with a long chain that wraps around the top of the plant pot, and ending with a star-shaped mesh that supports the bottom of the pot.

Ch 42. Check the chain length is right, by wrapping it around the top of your pot. If it's the right size, the ends should just about touch (as pictured, right). It can be slightly loose, but not too tight for the ends to just meet.

If your chain is too long, you can restart your plant hanger with a slightly smaller hook.

If your chain is too short, you can restart your plant hanger with a slightly larger hook.

Join your chain with a sl st into a ring, being careful not to twist the chain.

Tip: *To get the neatest result, I recommend you work all stitches worked* *into chains into the back loop and the back bar throughout this pattern.*

Rnd 1: ch 1, sc in same st as sl st, (ch 11, skip next 6 st, sc in next st) five times, ch 5, trtr in the first sc of the round.

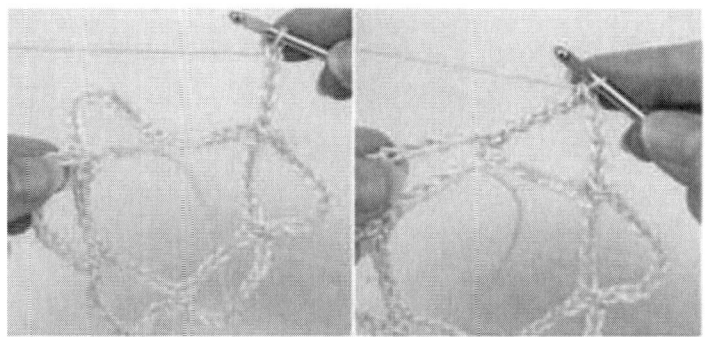

Above, left: The ch 5 creates half of the final loop. Above, right: The trtr stitch completes the final loop and leaves your hook at the top of the loop, ready to begin the next round.

Rnd 2: ch 1, sc in loop below, (ch 5, sc in next loop) around to last loop, ch 2, dc in the first sc of the round.

Rnd 3: ch 1, sc in loop below, (ch 3, sc in next loop) around to last loop, ch 1, hdc in the first sc of the round.

Rnd 4: ch 1, sc in loop below, (ch 1, sc in next loop) around to last loop, ch 1, sl st in the first sc of the round.

Fasten off and weave in the yarn end.

Tip: *You don't need to weave in the starting tail; you'll be crocheting over it in the next step!*

Top Border and Loops for Hanging Chains

To make the top border:

Hold the pot holder upright, with the starting chain around the top edge.

Fasten on by drawing up a loop in any chain just after a repeat point (pictured below, left), ch 1. Crocheting over the starting yarn tail as you go, sc in each chain around to the next point.

Tip: *Also crochet over the starting tail from the pot holder whenever you reach it.*

At the point, (sc, ch 5, sc) in next st (to make a loop, pictured below, right).

Sc in the next 13 stitches, to bring you to the next-but-one repeat point.

At the point, (sc, ch 5, sc) in next st.

Repeat steps 4 and 5.

Continue to sc around until you meet the start of the border round.

Join with sl st to the first stitch of the round, or, for a neater finish, use an invisible join.

Above, left: Fasten on just after a repeat point (where the loops of Rnd 1 meet the starting chain).
Above, right: The finished top border and a loop for one of the hanging chains.

Hanging Chains

The hanging chains will be formed from three long chain loops, joined together at the top. To make the hanging chains:

Ch 45.

Sc into the first (any) loop around the top edge of the holder (as pictured, right).

Ch 90, then sc into the next loop around the top edge of the holder to form a long loop.

Repeat step 3.

Ch 45, then join with a sl st to the first chain of your starting chain to complete the third long loop, being careful not to twist the chain.

Ch 1, sc in the loop below.

Working around the hanger, sc into each long loop of hanging chain (as pictured, below), making sure not to twist any of the loops before you crochet into them.

Sl st into the first sc (from Step 6) to join the top row into a circle. *Do not fasten off yet…*

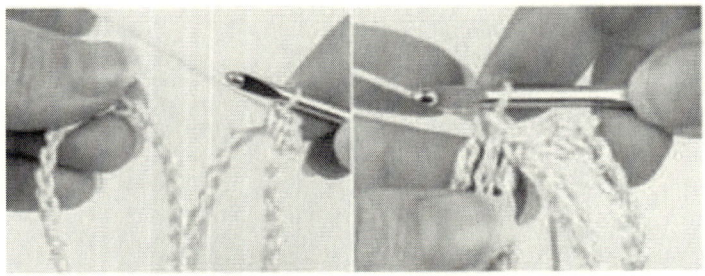

Hanging Loop

Ch 8 (or longer if you need a larger loop).

Anchor the loop with a sl st into a sc at the other side of the top circle.

Fasten off, and weave in all remaining ends.

Hang your plant in its new hanger, and enjoy!

Twisted Chain Bangle

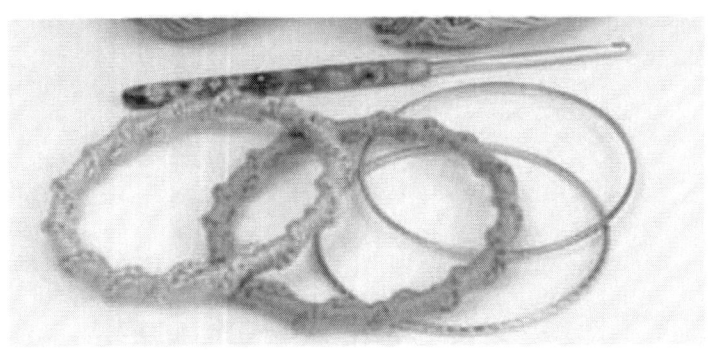

Terminology

ch   chain

sc   single crochet (double crochet for UK/Aus)

You will need…

Inexpensive bangles (see *Choosing Bangles*, below)

Crochet thread or yarn of your choice (light #3 or finer yarn recommended; size 10 or heavier thread recommended). The quantity needed will vary depending on your yarn thickness, hook size and bangle size, but you will typically need 5-10m for one bangle

Sample bangles used size 10 thread (KnitPicks Curio) and light #3 (sport weight) yarn (Patons Grace)

An appropriate hook (see the yarn's ball band as a starting point for the hook size, but you may wish to go up or down a couple of sizes to give different results – see *Gauge*, below). *Sample bangles used 7 US / 1.5mm, B US / 2.25mm and E US / 3.5mm hooks*

Needle to weave in ends (as small as possible, but large enough to fit your thread/yarn through the eye – an embroidery needle is a good choice)

Scissors

Step 1: Crocheting

Leaving a couple of inches of tail, tie the yarn around your bangle in a loose single knot (Figure 1). Holding the yarn tail along the bangle, insert your hook into the middle of the bangle (Figure 2), yarn over, and draw up a loop. Passing your hook over the top of the bangle, yarn over and ch 1. This will anchor your yarn to the bangle and give you a working loop on your hook (Figure 3).

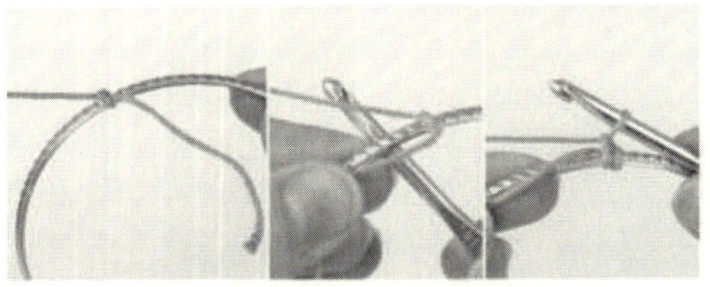

L-R: *Figure 1, Figure 2, Figure 3*

Begin to single crochet around the bangle and the starting tail.

Note: *If you haven't crocheted around something before, it follows exactly the same principle as working into a* magic ring, *except you work around the bangle instead of the ring! In other words, to make each single crochet: insert your hook under the bangle, yarn over and draw up a loop, bring your hook over the bangle, yarn over and draw through both loops on the hook.*

Checkpoint A:

After crocheting a few stitches over both the bangle and the starting tail, make sure your starting knot is loose and your stitches aren't too tight – you must be able to rotate your stitches and the starting knot easily around the bangle (Figure 4), or the next step won't work.

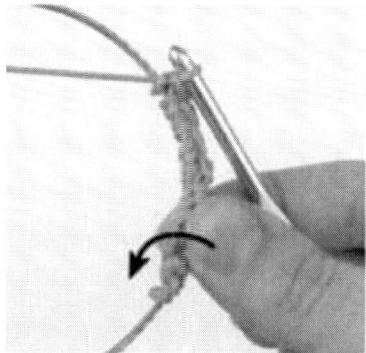

Figure 4

If your stitches won't slide easily over the bangle, unravel your work and start again, keeping your stitches more relaxed so there's more wiggle room.

If your stitches are sufficiently loose, drop the remainder of your starting tail and let it dangle, and continue to crochet around just the bangle.

Note: *Do not pull the end tight or cut off the remaining tail at this stage.*

Checkpoint B:

When you're about a quarter of the way around the bangle, stop and look at your stitches. You'll see that there are gaps between the bases of your stitches, where the bangle shows through between the wraps of yarn (Figure 5). (The size of the gaps will depend on the ratio of your hook, yarn and bangle sizes.)

Squash your stitches together so there are no gaps between the bases of your stitches (Figure 6). Don't worry if the tops of the stitches ruffle up – it will all straighten out later!

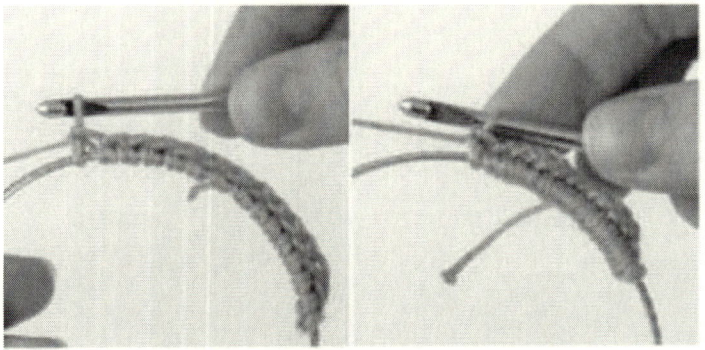

L-R: *Figure 5, Figure 6*

Continue crocheting around the bangle, stopping every inch or so to squash the bases of the stitches together. It'll take a lot more stitches than you think to cover the entire bangle this way!

Checkpoint C:

When you've crocheted all the way around the bangle (Figure 7), pull the ends of your crocheting away from each other to expose more bangle (Figure 8) – you'll find you can squeeze more stitches in there.

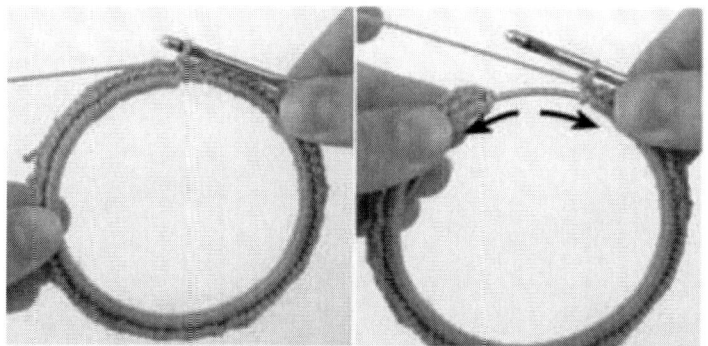

L-R: Figure 7, Figure 8

Repeat this process until you can't cram in any more stitches without overlapping previous stitches.

Note: *If you want, you can cut the working yarn now (see later for instructions) but I prefer to keep the yarn attached in case I need to squeeze in a few more stitches after Step 2!*

Step 2: Twisting

Now the bangle is completely covered, but the two ends are not joined. Starting from the hook end of the bangle, keep the final stitch in place and begin to twist the next stitches, rotating them forwards into the middle of the bangle (Figure 9).

Keep the twist moving around the bangle, always rotating the stitches forward into the middle of the bangle (Figure 10). When you've worked the twist right through to the starting end of the yarn, go back to the other end, start another twist, and work it forward around the bangle as before. Keep going in the same way until the entire bangle is twisted.

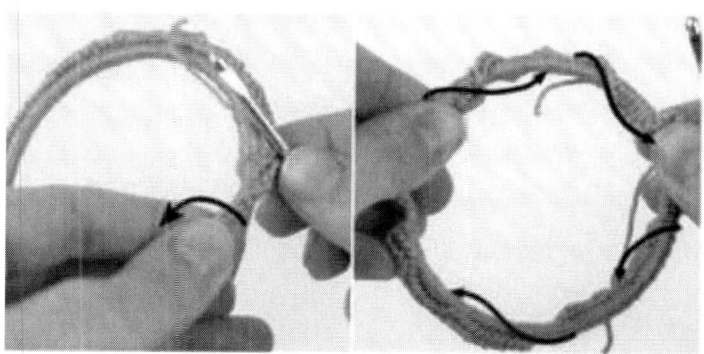

L-R: *Figure 9, Figure 10*

Note: You don't have to complete one twist before starting the next – try it out and you'll find a twisting pattern that's easiest for you. Just remember that, eventually, the first stitch you crocheted will have to be rotated as many times as there are twists in the finished bangle – there'll be a lot of rotations at that far end!

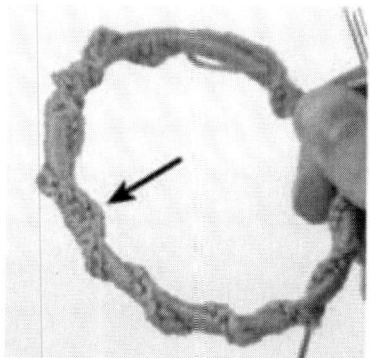

Figure 11

If your twist reverses direction halfway around the bangle (arrow, Figure 11), don't panic! It just means you need to keep that twist moving forwards towards the starting end of the bangle, by rotating the stitches towards the middle of the bangle. It'll even out into a neat spiral once you've put enough twists into the stitches.

Step 3: Finishing

When you've finished twisting, the V shapes that form the tops of the single crochets should form a continuous chain that spirals around and around the bangle. Take a good look at your bangle – this is your last chance to make sure you're happy with it:

If you're not satisfied with the level of twisting in the chain, tighten the twist by adding an additional rotation, or loosen it by removing one rotation.

If you find the bangle shows between some of your stitches, push the stitches together until they are tightly packed, and then crochet a few more stitches to fill the gap you've created.

When you're happy with the look of the bangle, tweak your twists (either add a little more twist or untwist slightly) until the V shapes at either end of your crocheting meet. Cut the working yarn, leaving a few inches of tail, then draw the last loop longer until the cut end is drawn through the top of the final stitch. Thread the cut end onto a needle, then use the Invisible Finish method to join the final stitch to the first stitch.

Weave in the yarn tail, pull the remaining starting tail tight, and then snip the excess of both yarn tails as close to your stitches as possible.

I hope you enjoy this pattern.

Made in United States
North Haven, CT
08 February 2022